THIS BOOK BELONGS TO

ISBN: 978-1-954961-35-7
Printed in the United States.

CHRISTMAS *Moments*

EXPERIENCING THE JOY OF THE SEASON

CONTENTS

GETTING STARTED

PART 1

A MOMENT WE'VE BEEN WAITING FOR

PART 2

A MOMENT WE DON'T THINK WE CAN LIVE UP TO

PART

3

A MOMENT MUCH BIGGER THAN US

PART

4

THE MOMENT THAT CHANGES ALL OTHER MOMENTS

HOW TO USE THIS GUIDE

This guide consists of four parts centered on "Christmas Moments" featuring the people who experienced the first Christmas.

All four parts include three separate devotions—short enough to be completed in one sitting, but filled with enough substance for a week.

Whether you read them on your own or together with your family, take some time to reflect and allow the Lord to encourage you through His Word.

In addition to the devotions are multiple recipes, activity pages, and Christmas-themed intentional moments you can do with your loved ones, whether that's family, roommates, or friends!

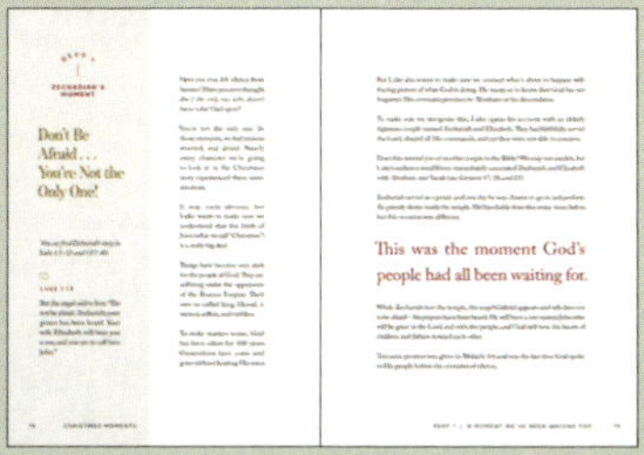

DEVOTION

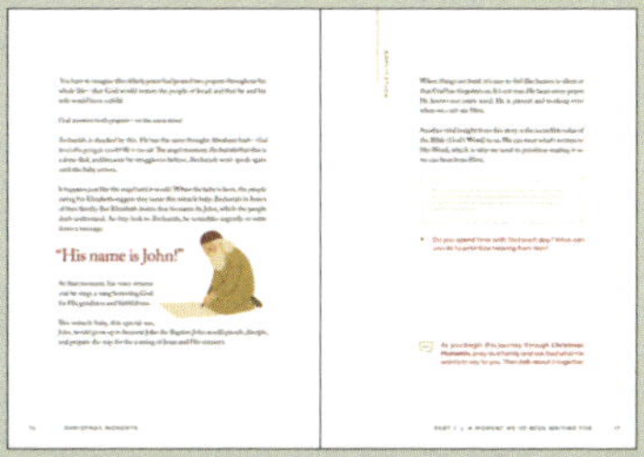

APPLICATION

PRAYER

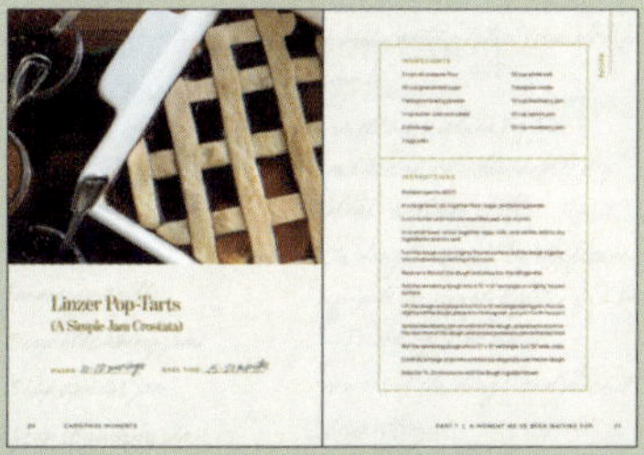

RECIPE

ACTIVITY

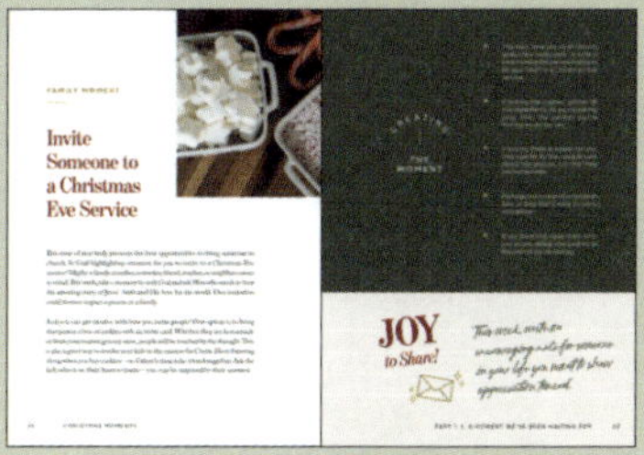

FAMILY MOMENT

✳ Is this an Advent book?

Yes and no. The term "Advent" comes from the Latin word *adventus*, which means "coming" or "arrival." Traditionally, Advent is the season in the Christian liturgical calendar that marks the beginning of the church year. It begins on the fourth Sunday before Christmas and is a time of anticipation and preparation for the coming of Jesus.

So, yes, this is an Advent book in that it will help you do all of those things.

However, unlike a traditional Advent calendar, this guide doesn't provide individually planned moments for each day leading up to Christmas.

✳ Does it cover the entire Christmas story?

Yes! Throughout the twelve devotions, we will read the entirety of both Matthew and Luke's accounts of the events leading up to and including Jesus' birth.

You may be surprised to discover these are the only two Gospels that include details of this part of the Christmas story. Because Matthew is writing to a Jewish audience and Luke is writing to Gentiles, they emphasize different aspects and characters while communicating the same story.

Throughout the book, we will dive into all of these moments, thinking through passages from both the Old and New Testaments that provide even greater insight into their significance.

Don't Be Afraid… You're Not the Only One!

PART ONE

A MOMENT WE'VE BEEN WAITING FOR

DEVO 1

ZECHARIAH'S MOMENT

Don't Be Afraid . . . You're Not the Only One!

You can find Zechariah's story in Luke 1:5–25 and 1:57–80.

LUKE 1:13

But the angel said to him: "Do not be afraid, Zechariah; your prayer has been heard. Your wife Elizabeth will bear you a son, and you are to call him John."

Have you ever felt silence from heaven? Have you ever thought, *Am I the only one who doesn't know what God's up to?*

You're not the only one. In those moments, we feel anxious, worried, and afraid. Nearly every character we're going to look at in the Christmas story experienced these same emotions.

It may seem obvious, but Luke wants to make sure we understand that the birth of Jesus (what we call "Christmas") is a really big deal.

Things have become very dark for the people of God. They are suffering under the oppression of the Roman Empire. Their own so-called king, Herod, is wicked, selfish, and ruthless.

To make matters worse, God has been silent for 400 years. Generations have come and gone without hearing His voice.

But Luke also wants to make sure we connect what's about to happen with the big picture of what God is doing. He wants us to know that God has not forgotten His covenant promises to Abraham or his descendants.

To make sure we recognize this, Luke opens his account with an elderly righteous couple named Zechariah and Elizabeth. They had faithfully served the Lord, obeyed all His commands, and yet they were not able to conceive.

Does this remind you of another couple in the Bible? We may not catch it, but Luke's audience would have immediately associated Zechariah and Elizabeth with Abraham and Sarah (see Genesis 17, 18, and 21).

Zechariah served as a priest, and one day he was chosen to go in and perform the priestly duties inside the temple. He'd probably done this many times before, but this occasion was different.

This was the moment God's people had all been waiting for.

While Zechariah is in the temple, the angel Gabriel appears and tells him not to be afraid—his prayers have been heard. He will have a son named John who will be great in the Lord and with the people, and God will turn the hearts of children and fathers toward each other.

This same promise was given in Malachi 4:6 and was the last time God spoke to His people before the centuries of silence.

You have to imagine this elderly priest had prayed two prayers throughout his whole life—that God would restore the people of Israel and that he and his wife would have a child.

God answers both prayers—at the same time!

Zechariah is shocked by this. He has the same thought Abraham had—*God, how's this going to work? We're too old.* The angel reassures Zechariah that this is a done deal, and because he struggles to believe, Zechariah won't speak again until the baby arrives.

It happens just like the angel said it would. When the baby is born, the people caring for Elizabeth suggest they name this miracle baby Zechariah in honor of their family. But Elizabeth insists that his name be John, which the people don't understand. As they look to Zechariah, he scrambles urgently to write down a message:

"His name is John!"

At that moment, his voice returns and he sings a song honoring God for His goodness and faithfulness.

This miracle baby, this special son, John, would grow up to become John the Baptist. John would preach, disciple, and prepare the way for the coming of Jesus and His ministry.

APPLICATION

When things are hard, it's easy to feel like heaven is silent or that God has forgotten us. It's not true. He hears every prayer. He knows our every need. He is present and working even when we can't see Him.

Another vital insight from this story is the incredible value of the Bible (God's Word) to us. We can trust what's written in His Word, which is why we need to prioritize reading it so we can hear from Him.

> At the end of each devotion, a set of questions is provided for you to reflect on individually and/or discuss as a family, or with a friend, along with space to write anything you want to remember.

* Do you spend time with God each day? What can you do to prioritize hearing from Him?

As you begin this journey through ***Christmas Moments***, pray as a family and ask God what He wants to say to you. Then talk about it together.

PRAYER

Father God, we believe You see our every need. We believe You know what we're praying for before we ask it. We trust that You are always with us and going before us. *As we enter this Christmas season, help us to hear Your voice and to know You more.*

WRITE OUT YOUR OWN PRAYER

Linzer Pop-Tarts
(A Simple Jam Crostata)

MAKES: *10-12 servings* BAKE TIME: *15-20 minutes*

RECIPE

INGREDIENTS

3 cups all-purpose flour

1/2 cup granulated sugar

1 teaspoon baking powder

1 cup butter, cold and cubed

2 whole eggs

2 egg yolks

1/2 cup whole milk

1 teaspoon vanilla

1/3 cup blackberry jam

1/3 cup apricot jam

1/3 cup strawberry jam

INSTRUCTIONS

Preheat oven to 400°F.

In a large bowl, stir together flour, sugar, and baking powder.

Cut in butter until mixture resembles pea-size crumbs.

In a small bowl, whisk together eggs, milk, and vanilla; add to dry ingredients and mix well.

Turn the dough out on a lightly floured surface; pull the dough together into a ball without working it too much.

Reserve a third of the dough and place it in the refrigerator.

Roll the remaining dough into a 15" x 10" rectangle on a lightly floured surface.

Lift the dough and place it in a 14.5" x 10" rectangle baking pan. (You can slightly roll the dough, place it in a baking dish, and pat it to fit the pan.)

Spread blackberry jam on a third of the dough, spread apricot jam on the next third of the dough, and spread strawberry jam on the last third.

Roll the remaining dough into a 12" x 10" rectangle. Cut 1/2" wide strips.

Carefully arrange strips into a lattice top diagonally over the jam dough.

Bake for 15–20 minutes or until the dough is golden brown.

DEVO 2

ELIZABETH'S MOMENT

The God Who Gives Favor and Takes Away Disgrace

You can find Elizabeth's story in Luke 1:5–25, 1:39–45, and 1:57–66.

LUKE 1:45

"Blessed is she who has believed that the Lord would fulfill his promises to her!"

We all know Christmas is a big deal. Beyond the commercial holiday and our family traditions, the actual historic event changed the world.

And as we're learning, the moments leading up to the birth of Jesus were also filled with supernatural miracles and the presence of God.

Imagine being Elizabeth—you've faithfully served the Lord your whole life with your husband, an actual priest in the temple. Being a priest's wife came with intense scrutiny and high expectations, but the Bible says she did it blamelessly.

But what Elizabeth really wanted were children she could love and train to honor God. Like so many others, she wasn't able to experience this dream. And because of this, she felt disgraced before the people.

That's a lot to carry. The expectations we have for ourselves and the expectations we feel from others can fill us with shame. It's hard to feel close to God when you live this way.

Elizabeth felt the weight of all of this. And then one day, when she and Zechariah are both elderly, her husband comes home from work unable to speak. This isn't the usual tired-husband silence; he literally cannot speak.

The people at the temple think he has experienced a vision because when he finally comes out, he can only communicate through gestures. We don't know all the details, but before long, this faithful, elderly woman was expecting a baby.

And she knows God has done this supernaturally, out of His love for her.

In the sixth month of Elizabeth's pregnancy, God sends the angel Gabriel to Nazareth to deliver even bigger news to her relative Mary.

Mary rushes over to tell Elizabeth the news, and when she comes through the door of their home, baby John jumps in his mother's womb. Elizabeth is filled with the Holy Spirit, and before Mary can say anything, Elizabeth calls Mary and the baby she's carrying blessed.

This is a wild story. The women in their neighborhood would not have believed it.

Two relatives. One, too old to conceive, the other young and unmarried. Now both are carrying miracle babies.

But miracle babies don't come without pressure and challenges.

Elizabeth experienced disgrace for her inability to have children. Mary would face whispers about being with child before marraige.

Both had to learn to trust God as their source, their provider, and the One who gave them purpose and identity.

These babies had bigger purposes than simply being welcome additions to loving families. The first would prepare the way for the second. And the second was the long-awaited fulfillment of God's covenant promise to redeem all people in all places for all time.

While filled with the Spirit, Elizabeth makes a declaration that was true for Mary but is also true for all women everywhere—*blessed is she who believes the Lord will fulfill His promises to her!*

APPLICATION

God speaks to us in different ways. Sometimes, He comes to us directly. Other times, He comes to us through someone else—a trusted voice who shares our confidence in God and His Word.

No matter how He comes, He wants us to trust and believe what He has promised. Because when we do, we receive His blessing.

God doesn't always come in the way or in the timing we expect. It would have been easier for Elizabeth if God had come and moved in her situation sooner. It would have been more comfortable for Mary if God had given her this news once she and Joseph were married.

But they leaned on each other to make sense of what God was doing because both of them trusted God by faith.

- Do you find it challenging to trust God? Why or why not?

- Write down 2–3 trusted people in your life who you know prioritize God and His Word. If no one comes to mind, what's a step you could take in finding one?

Discuss how you can encourage and strengthen each other as you move toward God's promises together.

PRAYER

Lord, we choose to believe Your Word. We choose to process with trusted voices who will encourage us and help us move forward in wisdom and maturity. Thank You for turning circumstances that can feel painful and discouraging *into opportunities for Your favor and blessing.*

A MOMENT OF SCRIPTURE

Write out a verse from today's reading and take a moment to reflect on it.

Christmas Word Search

- Tree
- Holly
- Wreath
- Nativity
- Manger
- Angel
- Star
- Candle
- Shepherd
- Snow
- Jesus
- Wise men
- Ornament
- Mistletoe
- Bells
- Joy

H	I	J	A	S	M	H	S	W
B	T	M	W	L	Y	H	M	A
K	E	A	T	D	E	W	N	D
R	I	N	E	P	W	G	I	I
V	Y	G	H	R	E	O	E	Y
D	N	E	A	L	W	K	T	V
M	R	R	S	X	G	I	R	P
D	M	C	E	T	V	A	W	E
N	G	E	J	I	A	O	O	L
W	R	M	T	E	G	R	N	D
T	I	A	R	J	S	G	S	N
Y	N	S	X	S	F	U	L	A
P	U	A	E	E	I	I	S	C
F	R	Q	S	M	J	G	X	R
M	I	S	T	L	E	T	O	E
W	K	E	F	S	V	N	K	D
V	E	Y	L	L	O	H	F	M
T	N	E	M	A	N	R	O	S
I	U	S	S	S	L	L	E	B
B	F	E	R	U	U	J	O	Y

DEVO 3

SIMEON & ANNA'S MOMENT

You Can See with Your Own Eyes

You can find Simeon and Anna's story in Luke 2:22–38.

LUKE 2:26

It had been revealed to him by the Holy Spirit that he would not die before he had seen the Lord's Messiah.

Some of the best moments of Christmas are when expectations are exceeded in profound ways. These moments fill us with a sense of wonder and hope, often moving us to tears.

- A family member makes an unexpected appearance on Christmas morning.
- A child receives a surprise gift they've been hoping for.
- There is exciting news of an upcoming marriage or new addition to the family.

Jesus said that even with all their flaws, earthly fathers do their best to provide good things for their kids (Matthew 7:11). But our Heavenly Father is perfect, and every good and perfect gift we have comes from Him (James 1:17).

God is in the details.

He knows and cares about the desires of our hearts.

When Jesus is presented at the temple, Luke includes two older characters named Simeon and Anna.

Simeon was a devout and righteous man from Jerusalem who was waiting for Israel to be restored, which is another way of saying he was waiting for the Messiah, God's promised Redeemer.

The Holy Spirit had told Simeon he would not die before he got to see Him with his own eyes.

We don't know anything else about Simeon, but we know God kept His promise. Simeon holds Jesus in his arms and sings a song of praise while Mary and Joseph stand there marveling at his words.

At that moment, a prophet named Anna comes up to them. She is now very old—her husband had died after just seven years of marriage—and she has spent the rest of her life fasting and praying in the temple courts.

Anna had been waiting for this moment through years of pain and struggle. And now, at long last, here was the promised Messiah from heaven.

Imagine the joy she felt. Imagine the validation—God had never forgotten her or given up on His promises.

These two humble servants remained righteous and devout throughout their lives because they were convinced God was good and trustworthy.

Two people who had every reason to feel like outsiders but now—in one of the most significant moments in human history—find themselves close enough to touch the Son of God with their own hands and see Him with their own eyes.

Luke includes this moment not only for us to remember Simeon and Anna, but to help us better understand the God we serve.

He sees.
He knows.
He loves.
He is
faithful.

APPLICATION

God is in the details. He's a good Father. He can be trusted. Every good and perfect gift comes from Him.

He's in the business of making good on His promises. He loves to exceed our expectations with His goodness.

Don't give up on the dreams He's put in your heart. Just because it hasn't happened yet doesn't mean it won't happen. He's able to deliver exceedingly, abundantly above all we can ask or imagine. That's who our God is.

* Do you believe God is a good Father? Why or why not?

* What is one desire in your heart you're still trusting God for?

Together, discuss something you're hoping God will do. What makes the waiting hard? How can you encourage one another?

PRAYER

Father, Your Word tells us that every good and perfect gift comes from You. We believe You give us everything we need for life. We believe You want to give us the desires of our hearts. But more than anything You give, we believe You are the true gift.

Thank You for Your presence in our lives.

EVERY GOOD AND PERFECT GIFT *is from* ABOVE, COMING DOWN FROM THE FATHER OF THE HEAVENLY LIGHTS, WHO DOES NOT CHANGE LIKE SHIFTING SHADOWS.

—

JAMES 1:17

FAMILY MOMENT

Invite Someone to a Christmas Eve Service

This time of year truly presents the best opportunities to bring someone to church. Is God highlighting someone for you to invite to a Christmas Eve service? Maybe a family member, coworker, friend, teacher, or neighbor comes to mind. This week, take a moment to seek God and ask Him who needs to hear the amazing story of Jesus' birth and His love for the world. One invitation could forever impact a person or a family.

And you can get creative with how you invite people! One option is to bring that person a box of cookies with an invite card. Whether they are homemade or from your nearest grocery store, people will be touched by the thought. This is also a great way to involve your kids in the mission for Christ. Have them tag along when you buy cookies—or, if there's time, bake a batch together. Ask the kids who is on their heart to invite—you may be surprised by their answers!

CREATING THE MOMENT

- The next time you're at church, grab a few invite cards, or write a note inviting the person God puts on your heart to a Christmas Eve service.
- If baking the cookies, gather all the ingredients. As you're baking, pray that the person you're inviting would say yes.
- If buying them is easier for you, that's perfectly fine—people care about the gesture, not that they are homemade.
- Package the cookies in a container, box, or bag that's easy to carry and deliver.
- If you have kids, take them with you as you deliver the cookies to the person you're inviting.

JOY to Share!

This week, write an encouraging note for someone in your life you want to show appreciation toward.

What Do You Do When Things Don't Go As Planned?

PART TWO

A MOMENT WE DON'T THINK WE CAN LIVE UP TO

DEVO 1

MARY'S MOMENT

When God Speaks

You can find this part of Mary's story in Luke 1:26–56.

LUKE 1:38

"I am the Lord's servant," Mary answered. "May your word to me be fulfilled." Then the angel left her.

Every young adult feels a mixture of hope and fear about their future. This particular season is especially filled with dreams of how life will turn out.

What job will I take? Who will I marry? Where will I live?

These are big questions that weigh heavily on us, especially with the added pressure of opinions and expectations of our friends and family. Whether you're looking back, looking forward, or currently in this season, you can probably relate.

Mary had a sense of where her life was headed before God radically disrupted her plans. Arrangements had been made for her to marry a man named Joseph. We have every reason to believe she was busy with all the excitement and preparation for her engagement, wedding, and new life with her husband.

Then, on an otherwise ordinary day, an angel from God showed up with a message that forever changed human history.

Notice the angel's first words:

"Greetings, you who are highly favored! The Lord is with you."

The tone is warm, relational, and celebratory. To be favored means to have God's blessing, to be chosen, to receive grace not based on what you've done but on who you are.

Mary wasn't ready for this. Luke tells us she was "greatly troubled." And she hadn't even heard the hardest part yet.

This favor from God meant she would conceive in her womb and bear a son named Jesus. He would be great, known as the Son of God, and would forever sit on the throne of David.

All of this would happen not by natural means but through the power of the Holy Spirit.

Looking back, we celebrate this moment because we know how the story goes. But Mary lived it. She had to explain it to Joseph and her family, having no idea how they'd respond. And she had her own fears and insecurities to overcome.

How did she do it? Two things clearly stand out. First, she focused on God's Word, and second, she talked about her feelings with the right people.

Mary didn't know when the Holy Spirit would put this baby in her womb. But she knew the moment she started showing, everyone in her village would be talking about her. No one wants to live that way.

She couldn't control any of that, but she could choose to put her trust in what God had said.

The angel told Mary her elderly relative Elizabeth (who had been barren) was currently in her sixth month of pregnancy. All kinds of people around Mary had opinions about what God was doing.

But Mary prioritized the voice of Elizabeth, a righteous woman of faith, and through her, found powerful encouragement as God spoke.

Clearly, God's message to Mary was unique to her, but there are great insights we can receive from her story because God speaks to all of us. How do we respond when He speaks? Jesus answers this question by saying that His sheep hear His voice and follow Him (John 10:27).

God can speak to us through His Word, during a moment in a worship service, or when we're spending time with Him in prayer.

Remember Mary's first reaction? She was greatly troubled. She had fears and questions. But she said, "I am the Lord's servant . . . may your word to me be fulfilled." That's the heart we're after.

The same way God met Mary and lovingly guided her through His plan is how He wants to guide each of us.

God speaks to us, and we have to work through our emotions and the opinions of others in our lives.

We would be wise to follow Mary's example. When we think we've heard God, we should talk it through with trusted voices. Lean into people like Elizabeth—people of faith and character who walk with God and want the best for us.

- What has God spoken to you recently?

- How have you responded to His Word?

As a family, discuss something God has been teaching or revealing to you. How did it make you feel? Did you tell anyone? How can we love and support each other as we learn to recognize God's voice?

When we think we've heard God, we should talk it through with trusted voices.

PRAYER

Father, thank You for the ways You speak to me and guide me—through Your Word, through prayer, through Your Spirit's leading, and through wise people in my life. I want to know You and to hear You. I want to listen when You speak. Help me to have confidence to know it's You as I *compare it to what You've already said in Your Word.*

WRITE OUT YOUR OWN PRAYER

Frittata
(A Crustless Quiche)

MAKES: *8 servings* BAKE TIME: *20-25 minutes*

INGREDIENTS

6 eggs

1/4 cup heavy cream

1 cup breakfast sausage (browned and crumbled)

1 cup fresh spinach (thinly sliced)

1 cup shredded cheese

Salt and pepper to taste

OPTIONAL: Top with thinly sliced fresh jalapeños

INSTRUCTIONS

Preheat oven to 350°F.

In a mixing bowl, stir together eggs and heavy cream, then add in browned sausage, spinach, and shredded cheese.

Add salt and pepper. Stir to combine.

Pour into a pie plate (sprayed with cooking spray first).

Add fresh jalapeños to the top if desired.

Bake for approximately 25 minutes (check at 20) until firm in the middle.

Serve with salsa (see page 51).

Salsa

INGREDIENTS

1 32-oz can whole tomatoes

1 small yellow onion

1 tablespoon vegetable oil

1 bunch of cilantro

1 fresh jalapeño

1 teaspoon minced garlic

A squeeze of lime

Salt to taste

INSTRUCTIONS

Peel the onion and cut it into quarters.

Add all the ingredients to a blender or food processor and pulse until the desired consistency.

Taste and see if it needs more salt or spice. Enjoy!

TIP: *If you want your salsa to be less spicy, cut the jalapeño in half and take the seeds out before blending.*

DEVO 2

JOSEPH'S MOMENT

What?! Are You Sure, God?!

You can find this part of Joseph's story in Matthew 1:18–25.

MATTHEW 1:24

When Joseph woke up, he did what the angel of the Lord had commanded him and took Mary home as his wife.

While Joseph is one of the most important characters in the story of Christmas, we don't know much about him.

- **We don't know how old he was.** At that time, it was common for husbands to be considerably older than their wives.
- **We don't know how long he lived.** He only appears in the stories of Jesus' birth and adolescence.
- **We don't know what happened to him.** Most Bible scholars believe that because he was older and the average lifespan at this time was significantly shorter, he had died by the time Jesus entered His public ministry.

While we don't have all the answers to the details of Joseph's life, what we do know is both extraordinary and inspiring.

HERE'S WHAT WE KNOW:

- **Joseph and Mary were betrothed**—essentially, betrothal is a second stage of engagement where final arrangements were made between the families.
- **While betrothed, a righteous couple would be exclusively committed to each other, but not living and sleeping together.** Therefore, it was a problem when Matthew tells us Mary was found to be with child. Since Joseph knew the child wasn't his, his assumption was that Mary had been unfaithful.
- **Joseph was a just man and unwilling to put Mary to shame.** In the ancient world, adultery was a serious betrayal; it was exposed publicly and liable to extreme consequences.

Joseph must have truly loved Mary because he resolved to divorce her quietly. We get the sense it wasn't an easy decision. He wrestled with it. He agonized over it. But ultimately, he made his choice.

Two things are clear: first, betrothal was a serious commitment because separating was equivalent to divorce, and second, in his sadness and confusion, Joseph chose to neither shame nor punish Mary.

Mary's pregnancy would have been a massive scandal. And in case we're not convinced, Matthew begins his Gospel with a very unusual family genealogy. At this time in history, women were rarely mentioned in these lists of family histories, but he features *five* of them.

The first four were well-known for their association with things considered evil, impure, or unclean: *Tamar, Rahab, Ruth, and Bathsheba.* Their complicated, dramatic stories marked by scandal or unconventional circumstances would have made them ideal candidates for the Real Housewives of Ancient Israel.

The fifth woman is Mary.

The angel of the Lord appears to Joseph in a dream, tells him not to be afraid, tells him about Jesus and His mission, and connects what's happening to a powerful Messianic prophecy in Isaiah.

Joseph had already decided what he was going to do. But God challenged him to do the opposite.

To trust. To serve. To lead. To lay down his life for Mary and Jesus. Not because Joseph was strong enough, but because God was with him.

Joseph was human. At some point, he probably thought, *Are you serious, God? I can't do that. How can I trust Mary? What will everyone else say? How can I be a father to this boy who is called to such greatness when I'm not even his real dad?*

But he woke up, obeyed God's Word, cared for Mary and Jesus with his whole heart, and lovingly led this little family through a dangerous and difficult time.

By the grace of God, Joseph's obedience changed the world forever.

We can see Joseph truly loved Mary. He couldn't have done what he did without love. But he could only love Mary this way because he loved God even more.

Joseph's love for God was big enough for him to overcome all his fear, his worries about their future, his personal inconveniences, and his own insecurity to raise Jesus as his son.

Remember, all of this happened *after* Joseph resolved to divorce Mary quietly. He couldn't do it in his own strength, but when God called him to obey, he did all these things, and much, much more.

We all have areas of life where we know we don't have everything we need. The good news is God doesn't ask us to serve and obey Him in our own strength. He promises to be with us and do in us what we cannot do on our own.

God doesn't bring us to these moments to frustrate us. He allows challenges to enter our lives so that we will lean into Him.

✷ In what areas of your life do you feel inadequate?

* How might things shift once you ask God to be your strength?

Discuss what happens when you feel like you're not strong enough to face challenging circumstances. How does it make you feel about yourself? How does it make you feel about God?

PRAYER

Lord, we are so grateful that You are not limited by our abilities or feelings. You see things we can't see and know things we don't know. *When we feel inadequate, help us to put our trust in You!*

A MOMENT OF SCRIPTURE

Write out a verse from today's reading and take a moment to reflect on it.

Remember the *words* of the *Lord Jesus*, that He Himself said, "It is *more blessed* to *give* than to *receive*."

ACTS 20:35
(NASB)

DEVO 3

THE BIRTH OF JESUS

What Do You Do When Things Don't Go As Planned?

The classic description of the birth of Jesus is found in Luke 2:1–20.

LUKE 2:19

But Mary treasured up all these things and pondered them in her heart.

While there are so many wonderful things about Christmas, the season is not without its challenges and disappointments. One of the most difficult parts of this time of year is managing unmet expectations.

If it makes you feel any better, it's been this way from the start.

Remember, there was no nostalgia or warm seasonal feelings that first Christmas. People didn't start listening to Christmas music in July. They weren't getting their decorations ready before Thanksgiving.

It was the opposite. They had to return to their city of origin to be counted for a Roman census. That's worse than a day at the DMV.

Now imagine it takes more than a week to get there. On a dusty road. Surrounded by criminals and predators.

On the back of a donkey. When you're nine months pregnant.

Are you feeling the Christmas spirit?

It's hard to imagine that Mary and Joseph did, either.

You know how the story goes. When they finally make it to Bethlehem, all the hotels are booked. There's no place to stay, they're exhausted, and they're ready to have this baby. Most first-time moms are anxious, triple-checking their hospital bags and making sure their husbands haven't forgotten anything.

Mary and Joseph end up in a shelter for animals. Most scholars believe it was closer to a dark cave than the rustic barn we picture. Whatever the accommodations looked like, it wasn't what Mary and Joseph expected or hoped for.

It was not the ideal place to bring a baby into the world, much less *this* baby.

- The baby who was fully God and fully man.
- The baby with the Name above every other name.
- The baby who would grow to become the man who would take away the sins of the world.

But it's exactly where His Heavenly Father wanted Him. If Jesus had been born in a palace, the message would have been clear: He's only come for the elite.

Because Jesus came into the world in the humblest of settings, He came to be with all of us. No one is excluded.

Mary and Joseph couldn't have understood all of this. They probably felt guilty for the circumstances. This was a huge moment. Had they let God down?

But as they had done at each step along the way, they chose to trust God.

They didn't take it out on each other. They didn't let their feelings determine whether or not God was displeased with them.

Most new moms and dads hope to see their family and friends after they give birth. Mary and Joseph most likely didn't enjoy that warm reception. But they did get a surprise visit from a group of shepherds who responded to an angelic visitation to come and see Jesus.

Here is the key to this whole moment. As Mary pondered everything that had happened, she treasured all these things in her heart (Luke 2:19).

The disappointments, the joy, the missed expectations, and the surprising new experiences—she treasured them all. How could she do this?

She trusted God. It may sound simple, but it's the same way any of us can find the joy that's only available when we choose to treasure all that God brings us through.

When things don't go the way we want them to this Christmas, we can either get angry and frustrated with God, or we can trust Him.

Of course, it's frustrating when things don't happen the way we expect. It's okay to be disappointed when our expectations aren't met. At the same time, the fact that things haven't gone the way we hoped is not an indicator that God's not with us or that everything is ruined.

When we're tempted to feel this way—and eventually it happens to all of us—we should follow Mary's example. Think about the moments. Consider what God might be doing. Invite Him to speak to you and to be present. Thank Him for His goodness in your life.

And then you'll treasure these moments, too.

✷ Do you remember a moment in your life when you went through something difficult? Maybe you felt like an outsider. Or perhaps you went through a hard season and didn't feel seen. Describe below.

✷ How did it make you feel then? Looking back now, can you see what God was doing?

Let each family member share their experience. How can you encourage each other to trust God more?

PRAYER

God, help us to trust You when things don't work out the way we hoped they would this Christmas. When we're tempted to be frustrated, angry, or disappointed, help us to see You are with us and that we can experience Your peace and joy. *We want to treasure each moment You give us as we celebrate Jesus and His presence in our lives.*

TRUST IN THE LORD

WITH ALL YOUR

heart

AND LEAN NOT

ON YOUR OWN

UNDERSTANDING;

IN ALL YOUR WAYS

SUBMIT TO HIM,

AND HE WILL MAKE

YOUR PATHS

STRAIGHT.

PROVERBS 3:5–6

FAMILY MOMENT

Christmas Lights Drive

It wouldn't feel like Christmas without—you guessed it—Christmas lights. They're what give the season that classic, nostalgic feel. Most of us can still remember the excitement of being kids, watching our parents or neighbors climb a ladder to hang the lights on the house. Once the lights were up, we knew Christmas was right around the corner.

What's even more fun is piling into the car to look at Christmas lights and seeing how creative people get with their decorations. And it's always more enjoyable with a cup of hot chocolate to sip on. Whether you do it with family, friends, or roommates, pick a time that works for everyone and head out to see the lights!

CREATING THE MOMENT

- Make or buy hot chocolate.
- Dress in comfortable clothes. If you have kids, have them put on their pj's for the ride!
- Play Christmas music during the drive.
- Bring a phone or camera to capture the memories.

JOY
to Share!

Christmas is a wonderful time of year to express gratitude for all that God has done in your life while also being generous to others. If there's someone you know who is in need, find a way to bless them this week.

God's Up to Something Bigger

PART THREE

A MOMENT MUCH BIGGER THAN US

DEVO 7

THE SHEPHERDS' MOMENT

God's Up to Something Bigger

You can find the shepherds' story in Luke 2:8–20.

LUKE 2:17–18

17 When they had seen him, they spread the word concerning what had been told them about this child,
18 and all who heard it were amazed at what the shepherds said to them.

You may have noticed that in most Nativity scenes, the shepherds are on the team: Mary, Joseph, baby Jesus, wise men, shepherds, and usually a few animals.

And if you've ever enjoyed a kids' Christmas play, you probably noticed that shepherds were an easy way to get more kids into the performance. Grab a robe, a sheet, a headband, and something that passes for a staff . . . instant shepherd!

The angels invite the shepherds to come and celebrate the birth of God's chosen King. We're used to this idea.

But this would have sounded crazy in the ancient world.

Shepherds had no prestige. It was a difficult, dangerous, and dirty job—it usually got delegated to the younger brothers as soon as possible. Nobody wanted the responsibilities of being a shepherd, but everyone wanted the benefits of the sheep.

Yet the Bible is filled with shepherds. Abraham, Moses, Jacob, and David all took care of sheep. One of the most famous psalms begins with, "The Lord is my shepherd" (Psalm 23:1).

Later in His ministry, Jesus would call Himself "the good shepherd" (John 10:11).

Sheep have no natural defenses. They don't have sharp teeth or claws. They can't outrun the things that come to kill them. But they were central to the daily survival of the community. When they got separated and were in danger, their only hope was the shepherd. And because these threats were constant, the shepherd had to stay close to the sheep.

For these reasons and more, shepherds weren't invited to celebrate kings.

Except in this story, they're the first ones invited.

The angels tell them not to be afraid because they've come to bring good news that will cause great joy for ALL people.

This baby, this Jesus, is the King they've been waiting for.

Most kings delivered good news to a select few who did exactly what they said. But this King was different. His reign would bring great joy for *all*.

We can imagine the shepherds were nervous—would this King really welcome them? But they hurry to meet Him, and once they find Him in His humble surroundings, they're so moved that they tell everyone what happened.

The story could have stopped with them, but it was bigger than them. The news of their encounter was so extraordinary that word spread throughout the whole region. This truly was great joy for *all* the people.

Whenever God comes, He's always up to something bigger than us.

This is hard for us to understand because we live in a very individualistic culture—*it's all about me.* Most people come to God hoping He will do something for them. But God always works in us to work through us.

At the same time, being included in what God's doing gives us meaning, significance, and fulfillment. But it's always bigger than us.

Maybe you feel like one of the shepherds. Overlooked. Forgotten. Not included in the big moments of life. We all feel this way at times.

But God sees you. He knows your heart. He knows what you're going through. He sees you right where you are. He knows your thoughts and what you're feeling.

It's important for us to realize this.

He wants more for us than to just be seen. He wants us to be included in what He's doing. And His goal is to get our eyes off ourselves. He wants us to think bigger. We're not at our best when we hyperfocus on our needs.

✷ Do you believe God sees you? Do you know that He has invited you into His mission and purpose? How does knowing this change the way you think about your circumstances?

Discuss as a family: What might God be doing IN you so He can work THROUGH you? How can your family think BIGGER?

PRAYER

Jesus, we know You are the good news that brings great joy for all people! We believe that whenever You're working *in* us, You desire to work *through* us. Help us to see what You're doing because *we know it's always bigger than us.*

WRITE OUT YOUR OWN PRAYER

RECIPE

Decadent Toffee
(A Soft Toffee Bar)

MAKES: 12-16 servings

INGREDIENTS

1 16-oz bag chopped pecans

1 cup salted butter

1 1/2 cups packed brown sugar

12 oz milk chocolate chips

INSTRUCTIONS

Spray the bottom of a 13" x 9" pan with cooking spray.

Cover the bottom of the pan with chopped pecans.

In a saucepan over medium heat, stir the butter and brown sugar constantly until completely mixed as one.

Once butter and brown sugar join as one, cook for 7 more minutes, and then immediately pour over pecans.

While still hot, pour the bag of milk chocolate chips evenly over the top and cover with a baking sheet until the chips are a melty texture. Use a butter knife to spread melted chocolate evenly over the toffee.

Refrigerate until the chocolate becomes hard, but do not freeze. Cut into squares. Enjoy!

DEVO 2

THE WISE MEN'S MOMENT

A King Ready to Meet with You

You can find the wise men's story in Matthew 2:1–12.

MATTHEW 2:2

"Where is the one who has been born king of the Jews? We saw his star when it rose and have come to worship him."

Another group of familiar Nativity characters in the Christmas story are the wise men. Christmas carols sometimes call them "kings," and some Bible translations use the term "magi." The term is used to describe teachers, prophets, astronomers, and even sorcerers.

These men were serving in the royal courts of kingdoms to the east—likely Persia, Arabia, Babylon, or Midian. There was a common belief that the appearance of a new celestial light accompanied the divine birth of a new king.

We don't know how many of these wise men made the trip. The traditional understanding has been three because it matches the number of gifts presented to baby Jesus.

What we know for certain is that the birth of every other future king had been a dress rehearsal for this moment. Nearly every culture around the world believed its rulers were legitimate because of divine endorsement—that they sat on the throne because they were either sent by a god or were a god themselves.

Wherever their journey began, the wise men followed the star to Jerusalem.

They were likely shocked to discover that no one in Israel had been paying attention to the arrival of this new King.

Eventually, news of their arrival makes its way to the ruthless and illegitimate King Herod and his cronies, who summon them to explain what they're up to. The wise men knew the Bible better than Herod. They directed him to Micah's prophetic word identifying Bethlehem as the birthplace of this messianic shepherd King (Micah 5:2).

This was not a casual trip. These men had studied the Scriptures. They must have pored over the hundreds of Old Testament prophecies promising the arrival of God's anointed King who would not only save Israel, but the whole world.

When the moment came, when the King—the One True King—finally appeared, they had to see Him for themselves.

After leaving Herod, the wise men follow the star until it settles over a home in Bethlehem. Surely they were overjoyed that after their long journey, they'd finally found what they had been searching for.

You can sense their anticipation. Like Simeon and Anna, they waited, they endured, they believed, and as a result, God gave them their heart's desire.

The wise men got to see Jesus.

Notice they don't find Him in the manger but in a house. Scholars believe this is because the process of spotting the star and traveling to Bethlehem had likely taken a few months.

They bowed down and worshipped Him and presented Him with gold, frankincense, and myrrh. While the latter two gifts were the most desired spices sold by traveling merchants, they probably don't have any symbolic meaning beyond being generous offerings that demonstrated their love for King Jesus.

There are at least two significant takeaways from this story.

First, this King was unlike other kings. Most ancient kings ruled specific territories—each nation or people group had its own ruler with defined borders. But Jesus would be King of *all*—a King of kings. Wise men and rulers from other nations would recognize Him and worship Him as their own.

Second, the people He came to serve—people who had been waiting for Him for generations—didn't even realize He'd arrived.

It's interesting to consider that you can find this same problem in Israel at both the time of His arrival (birth) and the time of His impending departure (Palm Sunday). It's a sobering reminder that it's possible to be surrounded by God's activity and still miss what He's doing.

We live in a different time and a different place, but we're not so unlike the people of Israel. If we're not careful, we can miss what God is doing. We can easily get distracted with the worries and cares of life and lose sight of the fact that all around us, God is doing things that generations of people have been waiting to see.

If we give Jesus our hearts, our attention, and our affection, He will meet with us. He's not too busy. Even during the Christmas season, He doesn't ask us for advance warning. He doesn't expect us to clean ourselves up. We can come to Him just as we are.

And we need to remember our King is not tribal. He's so much bigger than we are. He's the King of the whole world. People from every language and nation will worship Him (Philippians 2:9-11).

✷ Do you regularly give Jesus your time and attention? What things most distract you from being with Him?

As a family, talk about how you plan to spend time with Jesus on your own throughout the Christmas season. What could it look like in the new year?

If we give Jesus our hearts, our attention, and our affection, He will meet with us.

PRAYER

Jesus, thank You for coming to be with us. Thank You for being a King who is willing to be with His people. Thank You for living the life You lived and for the death You died on our behalf so that we can have a genuine relationship with You. *Help us to prioritize time in Your presence.*

A MOMENT OF SCRIPTURE

Write out a verse from today's reading and take a moment to reflect on it.

Seek & Find

Find the hidden objects in this picture!

- 2 Polar Bears
- 3 Mice
- 1 Carousel Horse
- 1 Goose
- 1 Nutcracker
- 1 Angel
- 4 Gingerbread Men
- 1 Rabbit
- 8 Bells
- 4 Trumpets
- 8 Candy Canes
- 4 Cardinals
- 1 Cat
- 23 Stars
- 1 Dog
- 3 Crowns
- 11 Bows
- 1 Tiger

DEVO 3

HEROD'S MOMENT

Great in Your Own Eyes

You can find Herod's story in Matthew 2:1–20.

MATTHEW 2:3

When King Herod heard this he was disturbed, and all Jerusalem with him.

You probably weren't expecting a devotion about King Herod, but it's not a mistake. While you won't find him in a Nativity set, he still plays an important role in the Christmas story as an extreme example of a wicked heart.

Herod certainly did not see himself as the villain in the story. During his day, he was known as "Herod the Great," either because he rebuilt much of Jerusalem and the surrounding region, or because he had a stellar marketing team.

He started as a political outsider, with no legitimate ancestral claim to the throne. However, he was a shrewd diplomat and a cunning opportunist. This explains why the news of the birth of a genuine king would have been so threatening both to him and all his political allies.

Herod was neither devout nor moral in his leadership. He installed religious leaders whom he could manipulate and coerce. He was notorious for killing family members based on his paranoid suspicions of treason.

This larger context explains why he attempted to manipulate the wise men into revealing Jesus' location. He knew the difference between right and wrong. He could talk about doing the right thing.

But he had no intention of worshipping this new King, because Jesus threatened Herod's place at the center of his world. It disturbed him and everyone around him. He was planning to do to this baby what he had done to his wife, his mother-in-law, and at least four of his own sons.

He ended their lives because he saw them as a threat.

Once he realized that the wise men had outsmarted him and kept Jesus' location secret, in his furious rage, he ordered the execution of every boy in Bethlehem aged two years or younger. Matthew's audience would have immediately connected this with Pharaoh and the killing of babies in Exodus 1–2.

The angel of the Lord tells Joseph to take Mary and Jesus into Egypt until Herod (and his murderous jealousy) is dead.

Herod is a picture of what happens when our selfish nature runs wild with no limitations.

He's a mirror that reflects the human tendency to pursue and champion our greatness at the expense of others.

He tried to manipulate his way to greatness. He was willing to do anything and everything to make it happen. He was deceived, and he failed.

Position, power, influence, and accomplishments don't make you great.

Calling yourself great doesn't make you great.

The only way to be great is to humbly obey the One who truly is great.

You are not Herod, but the temptation to be great in our own eyes is deep within us and all around us. It's possible to know what's right and to talk about what's right while still putting ourselves first at the expense of others.

If we're not careful, this can ruin our Christmas celebrations. It often starts with good intentions—we want everyone to be joyful, so we create an expectation in our minds of how this will happen.

Then when things don't go according to plan, we get frustrated and try to manipulate our way to the outcomes we want. This tactic doesn't work.

Jesus had the opposite approach. He said the greatest of all is the servant of all (Matthew 23:11). Even though He is the King, He said He didn't come to be served but to serve and lay down His life (Matthew 20:28). He said it's better to give than to receive (Acts 20:35).

✳ Why does it sometimes feel so hard to lay down our desire to be served and choose to serve others instead?

Discuss what it looks like to love and serve each other. How can we follow Jesus' example of true greatness?

PRAYER

Jesus, there is no One like You. You are truly great. Help us to follow Your example. Help us to not get so fixated on our own desires that we end up manipulating the people around us. That's not who You've called us to be. *Give us the grace and power to serve others the way You have served us.*

JUST AS THE SON OF MAN *did not* COME TO BE SERVED, BUT TO SERVE, AND TO GIVE HIS LIFE AS A RANSOM FOR MANY.

MATTHEW 20:28

FAMILY MOMENT

Annual Ornament Tradition

What is your favorite thing about Christmas? Is it the music, the delicious food you wait for all year, the decorations, or the gifts? Perhaps it's planning intentional moments or traditions with family that are treasured for years to come.

One tradition you could add to your list is to make or buy an ornament that represents a memory from that year. While it's a fun craft idea for kids, it's also a way to display moments you'll want to remember. Depending on your season of life, maybe it begins with "Baby's First Christmas," an anniversary, or a special trip taken that year. Over time, the collection will grow, and your tree will become decorated with cherished memories.

It also gives you a reason to pause and reflect on all the wonderful years together with your loved ones, and to take time to pray for them as you pass by your tree.

CREATING THE MOMENT

* If crafting an ornament, gather your paper, string, hole puncher, markers, photos, glitter, and anything else you would like to decorate the ornament with.
* If you or your kids would rather buy an ornament, go to a store and pick one out that symbolizes a memory from this year.
* After you have bought or crafted your ornament, place it on your tree where it's visible and keep it for years to come.

JOY to Share!

Around the dinner table this week, have each person say something they love or appreciate about another person at the table.

What Do You Want for Christmas?

PART FOUR

THE MOMENT THAT CHANGES ALL OTHER MOMENTS

DEVO 1

JESUS

The Fullness of Time

GALATIANS 4:4–5 (NASB)

4 But when the fullness of the time came, God sent His Son, born of a woman, born under the Law, 5 so that He might redeem those who were under the Law, that we might receive the adoption as sons and daughters.

When you're a kid, it feels like it takes forever for Christmas to get here. Why does it have to take so long?

Waiting is hard on everyone. God's timing is difficult. We don't understand. But the truth is, He has a plan—and it's always bigger than us.

Our comfort and convenience don't factor into God's timing, not because He's trying to torment us, but because there's so much more happening than we can understand. But the waiting is never wasted. God uses that time to shape and form His people.

Understanding and adapting to God's timing is a clear pattern throughout the Bible. In Exodus, the people of God waited to be rescued from Egypt. They waited in the wilderness. They waited to enter the Promised Land.

And remember, the people of God had been waiting during His 400 years of silence that led up to this moment. Scholars call it "The Incarnation"—the moment that changed *every* other moment.

- The moment long anticipated by faithful men and women for generations.
- The moment prophets, kings, and angels had waited to see.
- The moment God sent His Son, born of a woman.

Every aspect is perfect, intentional, and requires the fullness of time.

Jesus didn't merely arrive in the manger; God *sent* His Son with a strategic, intentional mission. He was born of a woman and born under the law just like us. He experienced everything we face and was tempted in every way, yet He lived the life of perfect obedience none of us could measure up to.

This is why He, the perfect Son of God, is the only One able to redeem us.

He paid a debt we owed but could never repay to offer us His perfect righteousness, which we could never earn.

It's God's perfect plan to save and restore the world. It could only happen one way. And it could only happen in the fullness of time. That's why they had to wait. It's why we wait today for His return.

And that's why the celebration of Christmas is so special.

Waiting on God—trusting His timing and plan—often causes us to question Him. *Has He forgotten about us? Does He see what we're going through? Does He care? Have we done something to disqualify ourselves from God's goodness?*

We're not the only ones to feel this way. You can find people asking these questions throughout the Bible, and yet each time, God demonstrates His goodness and faithfulness to those who put their hope in Him.

✳ Where are you struggling with God's timing? Are you wondering what's taking so long? Remember, we receive the promises of God through faith and patience (Hebrews 6:12). What have you seen God do in you while you wait for Him?

Discuss this together as a family: How does the story of Christmas give us hope and confidence that God is working even while we're waiting?

PRAYER

Father, we choose to trust You while we wait. Even when we don't understand. Even when we're frustrated. You have shown Yourself faithful, time and time again. You have proven your goodness to us over and over. Help us to put our hope in You and develop faith and patience *as we wait on Your perfect timing. We trust You with our whole hearts.*

WRITE OUT YOUR OWN PRAYER

THE SIGNIFICANCE OF THE NATIVITY

A popular piece of decoration you will find in many people's houses is a Nativity set. But it isn't just a decor item; it represents so much more than that.

Have you ever taken the time to wonder what each person at that Nativity moment was thinking? Many of these devotions have been spent getting a better picture of what those individuals experienced, but it's good to pause and reflect again. This wasn't just another day; this wasn't just another birth in human history.

The Nativity represents hope, love, and grace in the person of Jesus. If you're feeling a little disappointed with how this Christmas season has gone, take a minute to reframe your perspective and fix your attention on the very real hope that is found in Jesus.

This week, find a time to think about and discuss the significance of each piece in the Nativity set as a family. If you don't have a set, don't worry—there is a Nativity coloring page located on page 123.

Refer to the verses given in the previous devotions to reflect on each person's story or simply use the passages below.

While your kids are coloring the picture or as you put together your Nativity set, talk about the importance of this moment and what it meant for each person who was present.

- **Luke 2:1–20**
  (Jesus, shepherds, angels, Mary and Joseph)
- **Luke 1:26–38**
  (The angel Gabriel and Mary)
- **Matthew 1:18–25**
  (Joseph)
- **Matthew 2:1–2, 2:9-11**
  (Wise men)

Heavenly Cinnamon Rolls

MAKES: 20-24 servings BAKE TIME: 15-20 minutes

INGREDIENTS

DOUGH

2 cups whole milk

1 heaping tablespoon quick-rise yeast

5–5 1/2 cups flour

1 teaspoon salt

3 teaspoons baking powder

1/2 cup sugar

1 cup solid vegetable shortening

CINNAMON FILLING

1/2 cup salted butter, melted

1 1/2 cups sugar

2–4 tablespoons cinnamon

POWDERED SUGAR ICING

1/2 cup salted butter, melted

1 1/2 cups powdered sugar

1 teaspoon vanilla

3–5 tablespoons half and half

INSTRUCTIONS

DOUGH

Preheat oven to 400°F. Pour milk into a 2-cup measuring glass and heat in the microwave on high for 1 minute or until warm, but not hot. Add yeast and stir until mixed well; set aside, stirring occasionally.

In a mixing bowl, using an electric mixer with the paddle attachment, combine flour, salt, baking powder, and sugar until well blended. Remove the paddle attachment and replace it with the dough hook.

Cut in shortening until mixture resembles coarse meal. Stir the yeast and milk mixture well and add to the flour mixture, beating with a dough hook until the dough forms a ball and all the dough is loosened from the sides of the bowl.

Turn the dough onto a lightly floured surface and roll it into a 1/4-inch thick and an approximately 15" x 24" rectangle.

For the filling, brush with 1/2 cup melted butter all the way to the edges.

Mix cinnamon and sugar together, then sprinkle on top of the buttered dough. Starting at the long side, tightly roll up, pinching the seam to seal.

Cut into 20–24 slices. Spray a 13" x 9" glass baking dish with non-stick cooking spray, then place the slices of dough, cut side down, in the baking dish. Cover and let rise for about 30 minutes.

Bake for 15–20 minutes or until lightly golden brown. Cool in a pan on a wire rack. Combine the icing ingredients and drizzle over warm rolls.

ICING

Mix together butter, powdered sugar, vanilla, and half and half until smooth and creamy. Drizzle over cinnamon rolls lavishly.

DEVO 2

JESUS

There's No One like Jesus

ISAIAH 9:6

For to us a child is born,
  to us a son is given,
  and the government will be
  on his shoulders.
And he will be called
  Wonderful Counselor,
  Mighty God,
  Everlasting Father,
  Prince of Peace.

This verse from Isaiah is part of one of the most well-known Christmas passages.

You've probably received it on a Christmas card. As a result, it becomes familiar, which means it can also be taken for granted. It's worth slowing down to carefully consider what's being said.

From the moment Isaiah spoke these words, scholars have wondered who they described. *Who could fulfill such profound qualifications? Who could be a child and a Father? Who could be both the Mighty God and a Prince?*

Some have speculated that they applied to King Hezekiah. But even his greatest supporters would not exaggerate to this level. Others wondered whether they referred to Israel's greatest historic king (David), but he never would have allowed himself to be described as "God" or to receive worship.

Like Daniel 7, Isaiah 53, and the hundreds of other prophetic words given throughout the Old Testament, these words could *only* describe Jesus: the Messiah, God's chosen King, the One who would repair the breach between God and man, bringing everlasting peace to the world.

This well-known passage is far more profound than traditional Christmas nostalgia. It shows us the uniqueness of Jesus and what makes Him so special.

Jesus is so much more than a baby in a manger or a wise moral teacher.

You've probably heard the cliché, "Jesus is the reason for the season," but do you know what makes Him unique? Do you realize why He stands alone in history?

One brief devotion cannot begin to contain all of His greatness, but let's consider a few of His magnificent qualities.

First, the infinite, eternal, uncreated God came to us as a child. Think about that. Instead of meeting us in His unlimited power, He comes to us in His humility so that we can relate to Him.

Second, more than a king, a judge, or a ruler, He comes as a Son to model what it looks like to have a perfect relationship with the Father. This communicates the heart of His Father as well, who generously and freely gives His most cherished Son, not to a few elite righteous people, but to all of us.

This Son doesn't arrive in a castle where only priests and kings can see Him, but to humble, overlooked shepherds and wise men who traveled from other nations to worship Him.

Third, all authority of every government has been given to Him, but He is a righteous ruler. He does not control or coerce. He will not manipulate or deceive. He is a Wonderful Counselor. He leads people as the Good Shepherd—lovingly protecting the sheep as He leads and guides them into goodness and mercy all the days of their lives (Psalm 23:6).

Fourth, He is THE Mighty God. Later, He would baffle the town's greatest minds when He said things like, "Before Abraham was born, I am" (John 8:58). He forgave sins, received worship, and answered to God's holiest name (YHWH).

Fifth, He is so completely unified with His Father that they are One (John 10:30). He spent intentional time with Him every day. He only did what He saw His Father doing (John 5:19). Jesus told His followers that because they had seen Him, they had seen the Father (John 14:9).

And finally, He is the Prince of Peace. Peace doesn't come from a quiet night by the fireplace or a beautiful view of falling snow.

It's not from a lack of conflict or crisis in our lives.

True peace, the shalom of God, is a gift that only Jesus can offer us. He IS our peace.

This list only scratches the surface. You can read Colossians chapter 1 to find out more. Or consider what John, one of His closest friends and disciples, said at the end of his Gospel: "Jesus did many other things as well. If every one of them were written down, I suppose that even the whole world would not have room for the books that would be written" (John 21:25).

Let Christmas remind us that there is truly *no one* like Jesus.

APPLICATION

Celebrate all of your family moments. Bake and enjoy all the great treats of the season. Do the shopping and get all the gifts. Go see Christmas lights. All of these things are part of why we love Christmas.

But let's not forget *who* is at the center of all our activity. His name is Jesus. There is *no one* like Him. He wants you to know Him more deeply. He wants to become more real to every person in your family. He wants all of you to experience more of who He is.

✷ What is one simple thing you can do this Christmas season to know Jesus more?

Together, take a moment for each of you to describe one aspect of who Jesus is and what it means to you. There are so many to choose from. Here are a few to get you started:

- *Wonderful Counselor*
- *Mighty God*
- *Everlasting Father*
- *Prince of Peace*
- *Son of God*
- *A friend who sticks closer than a brother*
- *The King of kings and Lord of lords*
- *The Good Shepherd*
- *The Bread of Life*
- *The Lamb of God*
- *The Lion of Judah*
- *The Alpha and Omega (the beginning and the end)*

PRAYER

Father, thank You for sending Jesus, Your one and only Son, to us. We receive Him as a demonstration of Your love. You loved us enough to send your best—Jesus. Not because we deserved or earned Jesus' presence in our lives, but because of Your great love.

We choose to keep our eyes on You this Christmas.

A MOMENT OF SCRIPTURE

Write out a verse from today's reading and take a moment to reflect on it.

For to us a *child*
is born, to us a son
is given, and the
government will be
on His *shoulders*. And
He will be called
Wonderful Counselor,
Mighty God,
Everlasting Father,
Prince of Peace.

ISAIAH 9:6

DEVO 3

JESUS

What Do You Want for Christmas?

ROMANS 6:23

For the wages of sin is death, but the gift of God is eternal life in Christ Jesus our Lord.

How would you answer this question: *What do you want for Christmas?*

It's a simple question. It's the place most kids start when they think of Christmas. That doesn't necessarily make us materialistic or consumer-focused; it's just how we're wired.

Part of what makes Christmas so special for children is hope. They get so excited because of the anticipation of great things being delivered just for them. They make a list, trusting they will receive their heart's desire.

It's why we want to experience Christmas through the eyes of a child.

That hope doesn't go away. As we get older, it often shifts to the hope of anticipation, waiting to see joy and gratitude on the faces of our loved ones. Giving them the perfect gift is a tangible way to demonstrate our love.

We're chasing this moment. It's important to us. It's why we struggle to rest or feel peace until we feel like we have everything we need.

Christmas flows from the heart of God, so the true meaning of this season is loving generosity. Every good and perfect gift comes from Him (James 1:17). As Jesus said, it's better to give than to receive (Acts 20:35).

We all know the difference between an obligatory gift exchange where we feel the pressure to come up with something for the sake of tradition, versus a genuine moment of finding a perfect expression of our love that blows them away.

There is one gift that stands above the rest. Better than a new car, the trip of a lifetime, the coolest toy, or the latest tech innovation.

This gift is priceless—more valuable than diamonds or gold—but it can't be bought or sold.

When you're trying to find the perfect gift, two concerns come to mind: *Can I afford it,* and *Is it available?* In other words, *Is there any way for me to actually secure this gift?*

Romans 6:23 explains that the wages of sin are death. Wages are what we've earned. Wages are owed to us. As flawed human beings, we realize we're not perfect. This explains why we feel guilty. It's not because persuasive people manipulate us. We feel guilty because we are guilty.

But that's what makes the gift so spectacular.

"The gift of God is eternal life in Christ Jesus our Lord." It's a gift—we can't earn it, and we don't deserve it.

Eternal life is less about quantity than it is about quality. We will spend forever with Him, but it's more than life that never ends—it's *the* life we've been created to live. It's life to the fullest. It's the life that truly is life.

And this life is only available through Jesus. He's not one option among many. He's not only good to a certain group of people.

He is unique. No one else lived a perfect, sinless life on our behalf. No one else died a death we deserved in our place. No one else defeated sin and death through His resurrection three days later.

And no one else can offer you a perfect relationship with God, not based on your righteousness, but through His perfect obedience.

He is the only way we can be adopted into the family of God.

Jesus didn't come to make good people better. He didn't come so that spiritually elite people could get the information they needed to become more religious.

If you've never received this gift, this can be your moment. In your own words, simply pray, "Jesus, I give You my life. Come into my life and be my Lord. I confess my sin and I receive the gift of new life in God that only You provide."

Once you've received this gift, you'll want everyone you love to experience it, too. You can share Romans 6:23 and these simple thoughts. You can invite them to a Christmas service with you. You can pray and ask God to move in their heart.

Our Father is so good and loving that even the process of sharing Him with others brings us closer to Him.

Whether we realize it or not, He is what we truly want for Christmas—and every other day of the year.

APPLICATION

There is no greater gift for your family or loved ones than Jesus. This isn't meant to create pressure or make you feel responsible for their salvation—He is a gift and therefore, He has to be received.

You can't force it to happen. But you can serve the people in your life with His love and in His name. You can pray for them. And you can trust God to help them receive the gift of eternal life.

✳ Who are you praying for this Christmas to receive Jesus?

As a family, how can we love and serve people in a way that points them to Jesus? Pray together for the people you want to see receive Him this Christmas.

There is no greater gift for your family or loved ones than Jesus.

PRAYER

Father, every good and perfect gift comes from You. Thank You for the gift of Your Son Jesus, the gift of salvation, and the opportunity to be welcomed into Your family as Your sons and daughters. We're asking You to do what only You can do—*bring the people we love who don't know You into a genuine relationship with Jesus.*

FOR GOD SO

LOVED THE

world

THAT HE GAVE HIS

ONE AND ONLY SON,

THAT WHOEVER

BELIEVES IN HIM

SHALL NOT PERISH

but have

ETERNAL LIFE.

—

JOHN 3:16

FAMILY MOMENT

Read the Christmas Story

The Christmas season seems to fly by every year, and if you're a parent, it's easy to place pressure on yourself to ensure that the month of December holds memorable experiences for the whole family. But this means finding the time for these moments while also navigating schedules filled with Christmas productions, choir concerts, parties, decorating, shopping, and cooking.

None of those things are bad—they all help make this season feel special. But the pace of it all can easily distract us from the true meaning of Christmas.

This is why finding time to read Luke 2 is so valuable. Whether it's Christmas Eve or the next morning before anyone opens their gifts, go around and take turns reading the Christmas story out loud. Your kids could even act it out! It's an opportunity to slow down, express gratitude to God for sending His Son to earth for us, and to remember why we celebrate the joy of the season in the first place.

CREATING THE MOMENT

- On Christmas Eve or Christmas morning, read Luke 2:1–20.
- Whatever season of life you're in, you can start this tradition now.
- If you have young kids, ask if they want to act out the Christmas story.
- After you've finished reading, pray and thank God for the gift of Jesus.

JOY to Share!

How can you help someone feel seen this week? Consider calling someone to encourage them, buying your friend or coworker a coffee, or blessing someone with a meal who is going through a difficult time.

For More Study Guides

LEADTOWIN.COM

Connect with Jeff Little

@PASTORJEFFLITTLE

@JEFFLITTLE

FOLLOW ***@LEADTO.WIN***
ON INSTAGRAM